The Goats of Grassy Hill

Copyright ©2021 Heidi Morris

All rights reserved.

Know well the condition of your flocks,
And pay attention to your herds;
For riches are not forever,
Nor does a crown endure to all generations.
When the grass disappears, the new growth is seen,
And the Herbs of the mountains are gathered in,
The lambs will be for your clothing,
And the goats will bring the price of a field,
And there will be enough goats' milk for your food,
For the food of your household,
And sustenance for your attendants.

Psalm 27:23-27

All scripture references:

Holy Bible: New American Standard Bible. 1995, 2020. LaHabra, CA: The Lockman Foundation.

Not too far from where you live, a good-natured herd of gentle goats live peaceful lives on a small family farm. Together with cows, chickens, ducks, and guinea fowl they spend their days foraging brush, chewing their cud, and enjoying one another's company. Each of the animals on the farm has their own story.

This is the story of the goats on Grassy Hill.

When you picture a farmyard goat, what image comes to your mind? Is it a fierce-looking billy goat with a long beard and sharp horns?

Maybe you imagine a floppy-eared nanny goat with long graceful legs, chewing her cud with a tender gaze.

Perhaps you picture of horde of baby goats racing through a barn, gamboling and careening off hay bales, twisting and leaping in the air!

If these are the goats you pictured,
you can find each of these at Grassy Hill Farm.

The goats at Grassy Hill are dairy goats. They come in all shapes, colors, and sizes, because they are a mixed herd. There are LaMancha goats, Nigerian Dwarf goats, and even a Myotonic or "fainting" goat! Most of the goats at Grassy Hill are a mixture of Nigerian Dwarf and LaMancha goats, and are called "Mini LaMancha" goats.

LaMancha dairy goats are easily recognized by their tiny ears —they have no cartilage on the outside of their ears. Flora, and her daughter, Greta, have what are called "gopher ears."

Only a few of the goats at Grassy Hill have ears that stick out from their head, like Nellie. Although Nellie is a Mini LaMancha, the genetics of her Nigerian Dwarf heritage were strong enough to give her long ears. Her daughter, Luna, has short "elf" ears.

Squiggles is a Myotonic, or "fainting" goat.

Her ears stick out from her head like airplane wings, don't you think?

Squiggles really does "faint" when she is scared. Her legs stiffen up and she rolls on her side. After a few seconds, she gathers herself up, shakes it off, and rejoins the herd.

You may have heard that "goats will eat *anything*." Actually, that is just not true! Goats are really very picky eaters, although they ARE very curious. Probably the pickiest eater at Grassy Hill Farm is Bobo. He might taste things that are offered, or mouth a food wrapper, or chew on a feed bag, but he's just curious. As often as not, he refuses treats that are offered, *unless* they are his favorite: salted peanuts in their shell. That's right! He eats them whole, shell and all.

Ranger and Snowbell enjoy a wider range of snacks. These long-time friends especially enjoy animal crackers, fruit, carrots, and pumpkin.

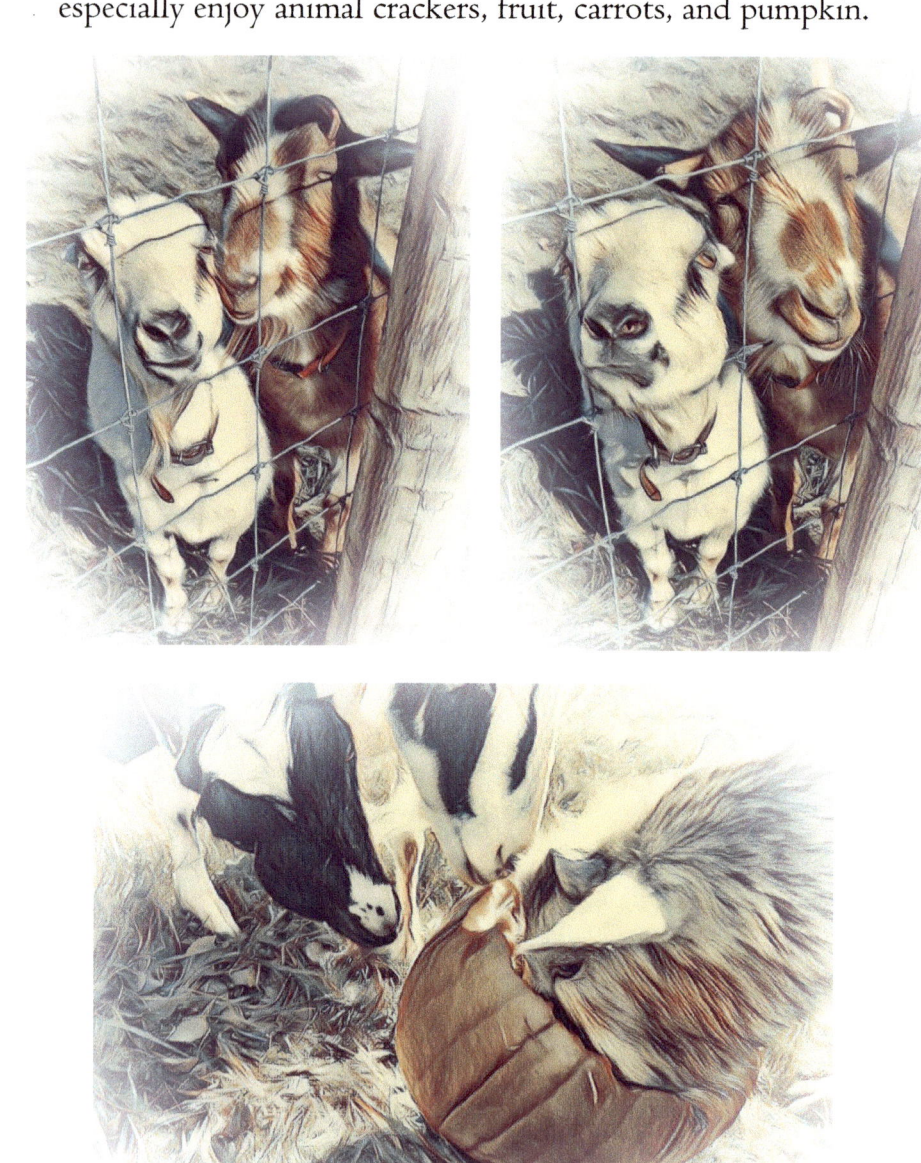

All of the goats at Grassy Hill enjoy leafy grass hay, low-hanging branches of oak and pine leaves, kudzu, poison ivy, greenbrier, and of course, fresh green pasture grass.

While the goats of Grassy Hill are mainly dairy goats, that is, they are raised for their milk, there are about 200 breeds of goat worldwide that meet the needs of their human owners by providing meat, milk, leather, and brush control. Many cities and towns hire herds of goats to control brush areas that are difficult to reach with mechanical tools. From the tiny pygmy goat from Africa to the large Boer goat that can weigh hundreds of pounds, there is a goat to meet every need!

Milk from the does at Grassy Hill Farm is used just like milk from cows. Yogurt and cheese, in addition to fresh milk for coffee and drinking are favorites of the farmers at Grassy Hill Farm. Most of the milk, however, is used to make Grassy Hill Farm's famous goat milk soap. With the special secret recipe, almost a quart of goat milk is used in each batch – that's about two ounces of goat milk used in each bar of soap!

Look at those eyes!

Unlike cats, dogs, or other domestic animals, goat eyes have a rectangular, horizontal pupil opening. This design allows them to have a much wider field of vision and allows them to take in more light.

Most of the goats at Grassy Hill have beautiful golden eyes like Ranger, the Nigerian Dwarf.

But some of the goats at Grassy Hill carry a blue-eyed gene, which is the result of cross-breeding with the Nigerian Dwarf breed. Biscuit and Lil'Bit have beautiful sky-blue eyes.

Hmmm….these eyes are different!

Udders full of milk and sharp, pointy horns are not a good combination. For that reason, most of the goats at Grassy Hill have had their horns removed at birth. Flower's repeated entanglement in the fence represents another reason that horns are often removed: safety. Flower and his pasture-mate, Fluff, have sticks taped to their horns to keep them from getting stuck in the fence. They don't seem to mind, and often appear to strut about, showing off their fancy headgear.

The Bible tells us in the book of Ecclesiastes that there is a season and a time for everything. Following the natural rhythm of the life cycle is very important for the health and well-being of all of the animals on Grassy Hill Farm. Just like on other family farms and homesteads, baby goats, or kids, are born in the early spring while mornings are still cold and frosty. The mama goats, or does, give birth in the warm barn on clean hay and spend the first few weeks with their offspring. After several weeks, all of the kid goats begin sleepovers together in the kidding stalls, which have been cleaned out and stocked with fresh hay and water. This allows the mama goats' milk to build up overnight so they can be milked in the mornings. After milking, the does are turned out with their kids, and there is a joyful reunion as each kid goat finds its mama.

The does who are in the milking program know their routine. Once the farmer comes to the barn, they line up, and are let into a waiting area awaiting their turn on the milk stand. Once there, with their head in the stanchion, they enjoy a breakfast of sunflower seed, wheat, corn, soybeans, and barley while they are milked by hand or by machine into steel bucket. After milking, they are thanked for their cooperation, given a pat, and sent on their way.

 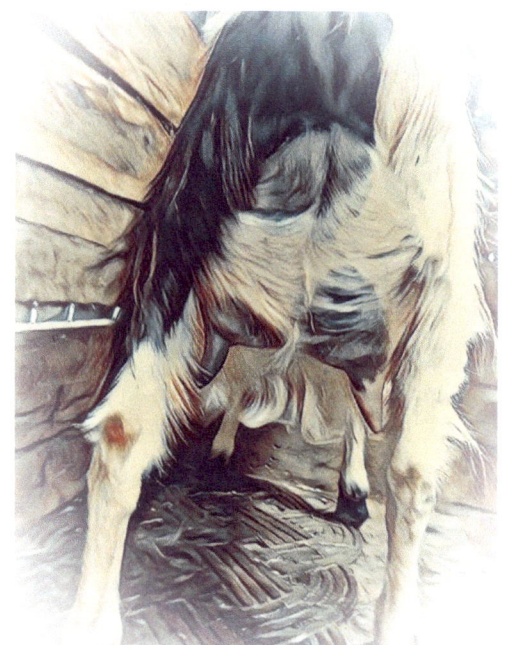

During milking season, the goats are milked once a day, right through most of the summer. Milk that is not used right away is filtered, chilled quickly, and stored in the deep freezer for use during the slower months.

Important decisions are made in the fall. Which does and bucks will be bred together? What family lines of goats produce the tastiest and most milk? How easy was kidding, and did the doe recover from the strain of kidding quickly?

When the final decisions on which goats to breed are made, then the does are placed into a special pen along with the selected buck for several weeks.

After everyone is sorted back out, it is time for a Goat Maintenance Day! All hands on deck as the farmers at Grassy Hill spend two days giving each of the goats their annual minerals, shots, toenail trims, and attend to other needs around the goat pens and pastures.

Winter is a quiet time on Grassy Hill Farm. Fresh hay has been stocked, and the goats enjoy quiet, lazy days soaking up warm sunbeams and enjoying their fluffy coats, grown thick and warm for wintertime. They spend most of their days snug in the barn, venturing out to explore and seek out fallen leaves or tender shoots of grass that may poke up from beneath the blanket of snow.

While the air is still cold, and sometimes when snow lingers on the ground, springtime is upon us, bringing a new crop of baby goats, usually in March or April. The goats at Grassy Hill typically have between 1 and 3 kids, with twins being the most common.

What a fun many days and weeks that is, with baby goats bouncing in the barn, skipping and leaping with their new friends, and resting when the mamas are out on the pasture.

And so the rhythm of life continues, and another year begins again.

We hope you enjoyed the story of the Goats of Grassy Hill.

Wouldn't you like to meet them for yourself?

*For every animal of the forest is Mine,
the cattle on a thousand hills.
I know every bird of the mountains.
and everything that moves in the field is Mine.*

Psalm 50:10-11

You can support the Goats of Grassy Hill and other family farms and homesteads by seeking out and purchasing products that they produce.

Grassy Hill Farm, LLC produces goat milk soap and seasonal items for sale. For more information, email: grassyhillgoats@gmail.com.

Thank you for your purchase of this book. All proceeds are returned to the Grassy Hill Goats to purchase feed, hay, veterinary care, and of course, peanuts and pumpkins.

www.ingramcontent.com/pod-product-compliance
Lightning Source LLC
Chambersburg PA
CBHW040344220526
45473CB00009B/2779